T

YOU REALLY WERE A 'WISE' GUY

Compiled, edited and written by:
Patrick D. Murphy &
William Bailey

FOR, TO AND ABOUT DAD ... A HEARTWARMING COLLECTION OF THE WEIRDNESS, LEVITY ... AND WISDOM OF DADS

Art nouveau-style line illustrations and decorative frames & borders -- from Dover Publications, Inc.

To send additional copies to *all* the fathers you know, head back (quickly) to your favorite book, gift and/or humor store.

Or, order through the publisher, toll-free, at **1-800-289-4843**

Library of Congress

Thanks, Dad.
You Really Were a "Wise" Guy.
By Patrick D. Murphy & William L. Bailey
Book design by Patrick D. Murphy
Cover design a collaborative effort by Murphy, Thomas Birney, Tammy Hurd and the staff of Electronic Keyline Graphics
ISBN 1-881139-09-3

Published by: Glovebox Guidebooks
Publishing Company
1112 Washburn Place, East
Saginaw, MI 48602

Printed in the United States of America
10 9 8 7 6 5 4 3 2 1

DEDICATED TO:

PATRICK LEO MURPHY

BENJAMIN BAILEY

THANKS, DADS.

WE HOPE

BEING A

"WISE GUY"

IS INFECTIOUS.

INTRODUCTION

Poppa. Pa. Old Man. The Big Guy. Pop. Dadda. Pops. Daddy. Dad. Whatever you call him, your father has been a significant influence in your life, in some combination of positives and negatives. (The same is true for Moms, but that's another book.)

Bill and I are no different. The memories we hold of our dads are fond and angry, loving and embarassing, irritating and loving. All are unique to us, yet very familiar to others. They help us capture a mental image of our fathers that becomes much more clear over time. The greatest thing about time, however, is that it allows us to step back from day to day interactions to enjoy a much broader impression of our male parent.

The result when considering this evolving view is a growing appreciation of the sincere efforts of our Dads – who took on a significant task of helping to raise us, armed with no training other than the memories they had of their own fathers.

Look at yourself. Perhaps your father did a better job than you thought. Maybe it's time you said, "Thanks, Dad. You really were a 'wise' guy after all."

- Pat Murphy

- Bill Bailey

On Being a Father …

Love, caring and nurturing should come from both parents, but typically, mothers provide more than fathers. Because of this, people tend to believe that dads are less important for the rearing of an emotionally healthy child.

Not so.

Dad will influence a child's identity much more than the mother. Dad's input defines to the child who he or she is individually and in relation to the rest of the world. This situation is most often recognized with sons. Literature, for example, stresses the importance of young boys having a "good role model." However, dad's influence is equally (if not more so) important to daughters. Messages sent by dad provide a mirror through which the girl can "see" herself. If dad focuses little attention on her, she could see herself as worthless, as not deserving attention from men.

Dad's verbal and non-verbal communications will tell a child if she/he is attractive, intelligent, hard-working, etc. The child's self-esteem is initially based on what dad said or did. This also has an impact on the child's reactions to others and, ultimately, a perception of his or her role in life.

As you enjoy this book, keep in mind these views "on being a father." Every statement or memory on these pages is a permanent part of the fabric of life for some individual …

thanks to dad.

Sandra L. Kroulik, ACSW, LMFT
Psychotherapist

Where Did You *Get* This Stuff?

All over the place.

1. Bill and I are fathers, so we get the credit (Or blame? Ask our kids.) for some of these comments. We also are the offsprings of great fathers, (See dedication page) so we shared a few memories of our own with you.

2. We sent questionnaires to a wide, diverse group of friends, relatives, business associates and acquaintances.

3. During our travels for our "day jobs," (Bill's in public service, mine in advertising and marketing) those sitting next to us on planes or in meetings were wonderful sources (particularly a kind lady from the Bahamas who gave me a real gem.)

4. Get togethers, parties and gatherings were also very helpful. We found that people get tired talking about the weather. We shared quite a few laughs as individuals remembered their fathers and their childhoods. A few not so pleasant but still telling comments were also gathered, and have been dutifully included.

The consensus - these guys who became our dads for the most part tried their best. Some were more successful than others. Quite a few were great. Hopefully you'll find a small piece of your dad in here..

P.S. We're doing similar books for Moms, siblings, spouses, ex-spouses and bosses. Check out the submission form at the back of this book. We'd love to hear from you.

Pat Murphy &

Bill Bailey

How Did You Get This Stuff?

Very unscientifically, via --

1. Conversations.
3. Hearsay.
4. Surveys.
5. Memories

We chatted, talked, took notes and, in general, did everything wrong in terms of scientific inquiry. We figured that casual research was okay anyway, since being a dad (actually, not biologically) cannot, in our humble opinion, be quantified based on any rationale thoughts.

Our sources told us that what their dads did or said. We did not independently verify these memories. They are good for those who shared them, and that's good enough for us.

If, for any reason, we inadvertently included something a father said that was something that someone else had already said earlier and has copyrighted, we apologize in advance.

Pat Murphy &

Bill Bailey

Dad's
five stages
of life:

1. *He gives me orders.*
2. *He gives me directions.*
3. *He gives me money.*
4. *He offers me advice.*
5. *He gives me fits.*

JUST WHAT IS A "DAD"?

The relationship between Dad and child is clearly a special one, uniquely defined by a myriad of experiences. Was Dad present at the moment of birth? Mine was not (It just wasn't done back then.) I've always wished he could have enjoyed the exhilaration of that moment as I did with my daughter.

Dads gain such wisdom and stature with age (the age of their children, that is). We all consider ourselves to be, at least in part, that from which we are conceived and are nurtured. One's mother exerts a profound and lasting influence ... but so does one's sire.

My Dad taught me many lessons without really making a pointed effort to do so. Perhaps the most important is the marvelous effect of **selflessness** in family life. Any father is immeasurably enriched when he is able to keep focus on family and not on self. The steady, consistent guidance Dad offered me is the benchmark by which I measure myself in my efforts to be a good father.

Family structure is in a state of continual change today, yet everyone has a Mom and a Dad. Some are raised by only one or the other; others by loving, caring adoptive surrogates. They have had an impact on us. We will likewise have an impact on our children. Future dads are watching us, waiting and learning how to be ... Dad.

James G. Royle, M.A.
Clinical Child Psychologist

The *real* pressure for Dad?

Hoping the baby didn't "poop" until Mom came home.

KEEP YOUR EYES OPEN

AND EARS CLEAN.

THAT WAY,

YOU WON'T MISS OUT

ON ANY JUICY STUFF.

When I asked
Dad
what a period
was,
he answered,
"The end
of a sentence."

My parent's fiftieth anniversary was a wonderful experience for our family -- and all we did was show up. Dad invested a year planning a trip to Disney World for Mom, my brother and me, our spouses and six kids, all expenses by Pop. We were not to spend even a penny.

His explanation, "I want to remind everyone of the good times you've given us. There is nothing I would rather do on my anniversary than spend it with all of you."

DAD'S ANSWER,
WHENEVER
I ASKED FOR
"SPECIAL" TREATMENT

WHATEVER
THE REST WANT
THAT'S WHAT
WE'LL DO.

I WONDER

IF CHASING

RAINBOWS

CAN BE

A CAREER

CHOICE

?

• *Dad, when pleased* •

I'M HAPPIER THAN A TWO-PECKERED GOAT

•Dad, on ice-covered highway•

THIS ROAD
IS
SLIPPERIER
THAN
SNOTTY
MARBLE.

•Dad, when overwhelmed•

I'M BUSIER THAN A CAT COVERING S---.

•*Dad, when food was "less than appetizing"*•

THIS TASTES LIKE SCORCHED KITTY CAT.

The
biggest error
you can make
is trying too hard
not to make
too many errors.

Dad,

describing

a local dignitary,

"He's a real pillory

of society."

DAD,

DESCRIBING

HIS ATTITUDE

TOWARD COMPETITION,

"SECOND PLACE

SUCKS."

The most fun part of family traveling was jumping on the motel beds, from one bed to the other, particularly the time Dad hit his head and cracked the ceiling and had to explain to the manager as he was writing a check for damages.

IT
MAY
NOT BE FAIR.

HOWEVER,
IT *IS* FINAL

I'm
watching
everything
you do
with a
fine tooth
comb.

Dad,
You *were*
right
after all

. . .

About *that*,
at least.

AFTER
I FINISHED
HIGH SCHOOL
FOOTBALL,
THEY RETIRED
MY NUMBER.

*THEY HAD TO.
I STOLE ALL MY
JERSERYS.*

THANKS,
DAD,
FOR ALWAYS
BELIEVING
IN ME.

My Dad's usual response, whenever I asked for anything

No, but thanks for asking.

Dad,

You always
said,
"You won't
appreciate all
we did for you
guys 'til
after we're
both gone."

I just said that
to *my* kids.

IF
IT WAS OKAY
WITH GOD
TO FOOL AROUND,
HE WOULD HAVE
GIVEN MOSES
THE
TEN SUGGESTIONS

“

Go
downstairs
and git me the
‘Whatchamacallit’
off the
‘Youknowwhatsit’.
And Do it,
Now!

”

IF YOU
DON'T EAT
YOUR
VEGETABLES,
YOU'LL GET
CRICKETS.

KNOW FIRST
WHERE
YOU WANT
TO GO

THEN
FIGURE OUT
HOW
TO GET THERE

And

just why

haven't you

fed the dog yet?

He's

a person too,

you know.

Dad,
Where do
magnets come
from?

Off the
refrigerator
door,
Denny.

BLACK

IS

BEAUTIFUL,

BUT NOT

ON A

PORK CHOP.

Spring Break at Panama City Beach, Florida. I'm sixteen, just one year from being able to *not* go with the family. I'm walking with Dad, totally mortified, ready to absolutely croak.

I'm in my best bikini. Dad's wearing sunglasses (from 7-11), plaid Bermuda shorts, knee-high black socks, wing tips, a white "T" shirt, and one of those caps with room for two beers (Bud Light) and tubes running to his mouth.

My friends look up as we pass.

? PUBERTY ?

That's When My Daughter Goes to the Convent

LOVE

IS BLIND.

THAT'S WHY GUYS

HAVE

ROVING HANDS.

DAD'S
LECTURES
WERE LIKE
USING A
SLEDGEHAMMER

. . .

TO
SWAT FLIES.

The Birds and the Bees

How did Dad explain "It"?

He didn't.

THE BIRDS AND THE BEES

HOW DID DAD EXPLAIN "IT"?

IF YOU AREN'T GOING TO MARRY THE GIRL -- KEEP YOUR PANTS ZIPPED UP.

THE BIRDS AND THE BEES

HOW DID DAD EXPLAIN "IT"?

SAVE THE PETTING FOR YOUR PETS

The Birds and the Bees

How did Dad explain "It"?

After being asked the "Big Question," he put on safety glasses and cranked up the chain saw *before* answering.

THE BIRDS AND THE BEES

HOW DID DAD EXPLAIN "IT"?

HOW CAN I
TELL *YOU* IF
I HAVEN'T
FIGURED IT
OUT MYSELF?

MAYBE
THAT'S WHY
I HAVE
NINE KIDS.

THE BIRDS AND THE BEES

HOW DID DAD EXPLAIN "IT"?

GO ASK MOM

DAD,

DESCRIBING

HIS FORTUNES

IN THE GAME OF LIFE,

"I'M ALWAYS

A DAY LATE AND

A DOLLAR SHORT."

Dad,

and his

reaction to the

many things

that went

against him

in life,

"It will build

character."

DAD,

WHEN DESCRIBING

ANYTHING

ABOUT HIS

CHILDHOOD,

"WHEN I WAS

YOUR AGE . . ."

DAD,

AND HIS

DISTINCTIVE

PRONUNCIATION

OF 'TH' AS 'T'."

TOOTH BECAME

TOOT,

BIRTHDAY BECAME

BIRTDAY, AND

THIRD ...

BECAME TURD.

DAD, DESCRIBING HIS FORMULA FOR SUCCESS, "BE ANYTHING YOU WANT TO BE. JUST WORK HARD, PAY ATTENTION - AND MARRY THE BOSS'S DAUGHTER."

DAD,

DESCRIBING HIS VERSION OF THE LADDER THEORY, "REMEMBER THE PEOPLE ON YOUR WAY UP, OR THEY'LL SURELY REMEMBER YOU ON YOUR WAY DOWN."

DAD,

DESCRIBING HIS

RECIPE FOR

PERSEVERANCE,

"YA GOTTA WADE

THROUGH

THE TRITE S---

TO GET TO

THE GOOD S--."

Dad,
I love you.

YOU WANT
THE
PERFECT MAN?
BUY
A NEW WALLET
AND FRAME
THE PICTURE
THAT COMES
WITH IT.

GREAT JOB
ON THE TEST.

WHO'D YOU
SIT NEXT TO?

My Dad's Request, whenever I was eager to get out of the house--

Before you go, here's a "short" list of things to do.

YOU'D BETTER
SMILE GOOD,
OR
I WILL
MAKE YOU WISH
YOU HAD.

THANKS, DAD.

YOU REALLY WERE
A "WISE GUY"
AFTER ALL.

If you
don’t
clean up
your room,
there’s
going to be
Hell to pay!

Dad always quoted
this Irish proverb --

"It is
easier
to seek
forgiveness
than ask
permission."

I DON'T REMEMBER
MENTIONING
ANYTHING ABOUT
DOING THIS THE
"RIGHT WAY."

I'M TELLING YOU
TO DO IT
"MY WAY."

WHY *CAN'T* I SLEEP WITH THE DOG?

YOU SLEEP WITH MOM, DON'T YOU?

(To his *only* daughter)

YOU ARE
MY *FAVORITE* DAUGHTER,
ABSOLUTELY,
WITHOUT A DOUBT,
YES SIR, FER SURE.

PAM

(To his *only* son)

YOU ARE
MY *FAVORITE* SON,
ABSOLUTELY,
WITHOUT A DOUBT,
YES SIR, FER SURE.

PHIL

EMBARASSING?

IT WAS HIS DEEP,
RUMBLING BELCH
AFTER DINNER,
WHILE HAVING
MY FIRST
"SERIOUS"
GIRLFRIEND
OVER.

EMBARASSING?

IT WAS HIM
CHEWING TOBACCO
IN FRONT OF
MY FRIENDS
AND SPITTING
THE JUICE INTO
A COKE CAN.

I HAVE YET TO FIND THE SCHOOLHOUSE DAD SAID HE WENT TO WHERE HE HAD TO WALK, BAREFOOT, TEN MILES EACH WAY, UPHILL BOTH WAYS, IN A DRIVING (RAIN OR SNOWSTORM), ON A ROAD MADE OF RAZOR SHARP, VOLCANIC GRAVEL.

Son, Mom wanted to name you Buford.

Seriously.

KIDS ARE LIKE
HEMORRHOIDS.

EVEN
THE GOOD ONES
ARE A PAIN
IN THE BUTT.

In virtually
any contest,
old age
& treachery
will get
the better
of youth
& idealism.

DAD
THOUGHT NOTHING
OF BARGING
INTO THE BATHROOM
WHILE I WAS
"IN ACTION."

I WONDER ...
IF DAD EVER KNEW
MOM WAS ALWAYS
TELLING US TO
TELL HIM SOMETHING
COST $25 LESS THAN
IT REALLY DID?

Dad,

You always complained of painful burning and itching.

Now I know what you mean.

As a youth,
Dad told us he had
three questions
of utmost concern
to him:
"Are we almost done?"
"What time is recess?"
"Where are the cookies?"

Come to think of it,
not much has changed.

Hey! You Think I Fell Off the Christmas Tree Yesterday?

ANNOY

YOUR ENEMIES

BEST

BY

FORGIVING

THEM.

Dad,

That gross
"pull my
thumb and
make me
fart" routine?

I do it to my
kids now.

Dad?
Why are we Catholic?
(Emphatically)
Don't even ask.
We were born Catholic.
Our family's *always*
been Catholic.
We will *always* be
Catholic.
We, er, aah,...
Oh, G - damn it!
Because I say so!

WHEN
A GIRL
THROWS A SPITBALL
AT YOU FIRST,
THAT THERE IS
ABSOLUTE PROOF
THAT SHE IS
IN LOVE WITH YOU.

Your Nose *Isn't* Big. Your Head is Just a Little Small

We are so Broke, We Can't Even Afford to Pay Attention

YOU KIDS WOULD SCREW UP A TWO CAR FUNERAL.

• GOD •
IS
SOCIALLY CORRECT,
ALL POWERFUL,
AND
HOLDS THE MORTGAGE
ON THE
WHOLE DARN PLANET.
• SANTA •
ON THE OTHER HAND,
KNOWS
WHEN YOU'VE BEEN
NAUGHTY.

Same S---, Different Day

BUT, DAD. JIMMY HAS ONE!

KEEP
YOUR EYES
SHUT
AND
YOUR MOUTH
OPEN.

THE
FLOGGING
WILL
CONTINUE
UNTIL
MORALE
IMPROVES
AROUND
HERE.

So many
to spank.
So little
time.

WHEN YOU HAVE
YOUR OWN HOME,
AND YOUR OWN CHILDREN,
AND YOUR OWN MONEY,
AND YOUR OWN BILLS,
YOU CAN MAKE
YOUR OWN DECISIONS.

UNTIL THEN . . .

IF YOU'RE GOING TO TAKE THE TIME TO DO A JOB, JUST BE SURE TO TAKE ENOUGH TIME TO

DO IT RIGHT.

Are ‘We’ Having Fun Yet

?

I Like
You Kids
Best 'Cuz
You Last
Longer
Than Pets.

“Don’t sit on cement, or you’ll get piles.”

I'm Flunking the School of Hard Knocks

THIS IS
NO
ORDINARY
HUMAN
WITH WHOM
YOU ARE
DEALING.

DAD
WAS ALL HAWK
AND NO SPIT
UNTIL
THE SURGERY.

Those that fail
to learn from History
usually
aren't doing well
in English either.

Because
***I* said so.**

• Don't •

Wish Too

Hard.

You May Just

Get Him.

• Do •

As I Say,

Not

As I Do.

• DON'T •

PUT ANYTHING

BIGGER THAN

YOUR ELBOW IN

THAT HOLE.

•Do•

Your

Homework.

You Have to

Support Me

When I'm Old

• Don't •

Even Think of

Buying It,

Unless You

Can't Think

of Living

Without It

• Don't •

Run Through a Sprinkler, or You'll Get Polio.

•Don't•

Even Think of

Going Out

Until You Say

You're Sorry

to

Your Brother.

•Don't Run Around Like a Chicken with Its Head Cut Off•

•Don't•

Even Think of Borrowing the Car.

As my friends
sat around,
telling stories,
Dad would listen in.

When
something
was particularly
interesting (to him),
he'd yell out,
"Well, Shit, Fart
and Bark
at the Moon!"

Why?

Is it so hard for Dad to say he loves me?

My Dad
was absolutely *great*
at Trivial Pursuit.

He seemed
to know answers
to questions
I didn't know
had even been asked.

It's Nice
to be Important,

But
It's more Important
to be Nice.

AFTER

FIVE BEERS,

DAD WAS ALWAYS

THE FIRST TO

VOLUNTEER

TO PUT OUT

THE CAMP FIRE.

WHY ARE GAS STATION REST ROOMS LOCKED FOR YOUR CONVENIENCE?

My parents lived in a different city, two hours away. After a really bad day in my personal life, I happened to talk to them on the phone. I put up my cheeriest, perkiest front, told a few jokes and, in general, "covered the hurt." This was about 4 P.M.

At 6:30, there was a knock at my door. Dad and Mom were standing there, said they just happened to be in the neighboorhood and figured I wanted a burger.

Afteward, I asked, "Okay, so what's the story?" Dad answered, "Well, we could tell from your voice that you needed someone to talk to, so we decided that a little drive before stopping for dinner would be a good idea."

Not good … great!

I KNOW NOW . . .

MY CHILDREN

RECEIVEDAN EXCESSIVE

AMOUNTOF FLOURIDE

AS YOUNGSTERS.

EVEN WHEN YOU FALL ON YOUR FACE, YOU'RE STILL MOVING FORWARD.

ALWAYS WEAR
CLEAN UNDERWEAR.

YOU NEVER KNOW
WHEN YOU'RE
GOING TO BE
IN AN ACCIDENT.

ALWAYS WEAR
UNDERWEAR
OR THAT THING
WILL BEAT YOU
TO DEATH.

THOSE
WHO LIVE
IN GLASS HOUSES
. . .
CAN SURE SEE
A LOT OF STUFF.

My Dad had an explosive temper, which was more funny than sad since he always unleashed it on inanimate objects … until I brought my final geography paper for him to sign. He gasped at the large "F" on the front, threw the paper to the floor and began berating me for my laziness, lack of initiative, etc. As he paced back and forth, he reached the crescendo of his tirade, but his anger had not yet peaked. Looking for anything to attack, he lunged for an envelope laying on his desk. He grabbed it, shook it at me and yelled, "And, if I ever see another "F" on *any* of your papers, I'll rip it to pieces, just like this!" He tore the envelope, crumbled the shreds and flung them into the fireplace, where they quickly flashed into a brilliant display. A brief silence was followed by a gasp escaping from Dad. He reached out helplessly to the glowing logs and fluttering scraps of blackened paper gently wafting skyward in the warm, thermal embrace of the rising smoke.
… all that was left of his paycheck.

DAD,
THANKS
FOR ALWAYS
SEEING
AND SHARING
THE HUMOR
IN THINGS.

My Father

by Michael Kroulik

Summer

His hands tightly
grip the bat.
He stands poised,
waiting for the pitch.
His muscles tense.
Striding forward,
his muscles relax.
With full force
he strikes the ball.
He runs to first
and hits the bag.
A small cloud of dust
congregates in the air above..
Rounding the bag
his opponents throw the ball.
toward first base.
He dives back
just in time.
Standing up, he brushes
away the dirt
on his uniform.
He explodes with pride
as his teammates congratulate him.

Winter

He stands at the net
ready to jump.
His muscles tense.
His teammate bumps the ball
to his wife who sends
the ball back up toward him.
It's over his head.
He times the jump
as he stares at the
slowly rotating ball in mid-air.
He winds up,
strikes the ball
with his open hand,
sending the ball shooting
past his diving opponents.
As the ball hits the
hard gymnasium floor
he explodes with pride
as his teammates congratulate him.

THE ROLE OF FATHER ...

THE ROLE ONE PLAYS IS DEFINED BY OTHERS

The role of a father is no different. It is defined for the male by his father, or by significant males during his childhood, through professionals who pontificate in the media or during instructional situations. It is also defined by one's spouse (who believes her husband should complement *her* actions.)

THE ROLE IS DEFINED BY CHILDREN

A child's is the voice to whom dad should listen. This is the voice that best describes what the child needs. This is the voice that will carry information for a lifetime. What a father says today is often the voice receiving the least attention.

FATHERS, LISTEN TO YOUR CHILDREN

They usually aren't as overt or assertive as others demanding attention. The payback is not tangible, nor is it always immediate. Children are too easily ignored or put off. Their requests come in quiet ways.

Listen. *They* will define your role.

Thomas P. West, ACSW
Psychotherapist

More Submissions Needed

More. More. More.

We need more submissions

HEARTLINES ® is a series of books celebrating and exploring the interactions of people in different "living" situations. This book (spotlighting Dads) is the first in an enjoyable, provocative series. Future books are being prepared, even as you read.

We'd love to get a snippet or two or more from you, on any or all of the subjects listed below. Send us your notes. We'll do our best to include your memories. We can't pay anything, but you will have the satisfaction of knowing that a cherished (or infamous) memory will forever be a part of printing lore.

How to Contact Us

Hard copy to: HEARTLINES C/O
1112 Washburn Place, East
Saginaw, MI 48602

E-mail: If you're connected to the Internet, e-mail
your snippets to Pat Murphy*
I'm on **CRIS,*
***Information & Entertainment Network**.*
My Internet address is:
Murph@cris.com *[no spaces]*

Titles & (Subjects) of Future **HEARTLINES** Books:

A. Thanks, Mom. You are a 'Smart' Person (Moms)
B. Honey, You're the BEST ! (Husbands)
C. Dear, You're the BEST ! (Wives)
D. Take my Ex, Please ! (Ex-spouses)
E. I'm Gonna Tell ! (Siblings)
F A New Theory of Relativity (aunts, uncles, cousins)
G Boss, You're the BEST ! (Superiors)